Rosita

Little Rose

JOSUE RIOS

PAGE PUBLISHING
Conneaut Lake, PA

First originally published by Page Publishing 2023

ISBN 979-8-88793-383-2 (pbk)
ISBN 979-8-88793-390-0 (digital)

Printed in the United States of America

To Margo. To forgive is courageous because you
are confronting conflictive emotions.

Acknowledgements

I'd first off like to thank God for the writing ability He has given me, I often wonder where I'd be had I never started writing again. Thank you to my mother and siblings for your love and support. Thank you to the homies, y'all know who you are. All of you are pillars to my sanity. And a special thank you to Wendy Urbina for my cover drawing, thank you for help bringing my vision to life! And last but not least, I'd like to thank the Manassas City library staff for their help and support throughout the publication process.

Inspired by Nature

The Sun and the Moon

The sun and the moon were once best friends.
When the sun would get together with the rest of
the stars, it would invite the moon to attend.
Before the earth was formed, and before the sun and the
moon apart from each other were tragically torn.
The sun and the moon were always together. They
often said that they would be together forever.
Then one day the sun and the moon got into an argument
over who shined brighter. The argument grew so intense that
they said that they didn't want to see each other any longer.
Before the moon left, the moon yelled to the sun, "I will shine
brighter than you!" The sun grew awfully sad for it knew once
they were apart, the moonlight would cease to continue.
Time went by, and the moon slowly and painfully
realized it could no longer shine.
From a distance, stars passed by. They saw the
moon was cold, and it would often cry.
The moon told the stars to tell the sun it was sorry,
so the stars did, and the sun said, "I can't bear
the thought of the moon being lonely."
So the sun told the stars to tell the moon to come
back to the formless earth. The stars did so, and when
the moon saw the sun, it said, "I know I said some
mean things, but I'm sorry for what it's worth."

The sun said, "I don't think we can continue to be together
like we used to, but every day I want to continue to see you.
So take your place on the opposite side of the world, and
you will always shine with me as bright as a pearl."
So the moon did as it was told, and every day since, the moon
danced as it revolved around the sun and never again grew cold.

Little Rose

Little rose I believe in you, throughout history
beauties like yours have been very few.
Due to the amount of times you've been trampled on,
you should have many thorns, but you are without
any even though your heart has been torn.
You've come a long way from being a little flower, for
you've absorbed all the mystical spring showers.
Little rose without thorns, breathtaking
beauty since the day you were born.
Little rose, believe in yourself; the day you
touched my heart will forever be felt.
Little rose, little rose, with beauty from your head to your toes.
If I were to decompose, your beauty would live on, I suppose.
Little rose without thorns, surviving even
the most relentless of storms.

Magenta Skies

Colorful magenta skies, as the sun above us radiates and flies.
The sky is a canvas of a painted portrait; it
is a unique and detailed sunset.
Enormous pillowish clouds hover, complimenting
the majestic magenta colors.
A unique and not so distant sun, this work of
art being painted must have been fun.
Magenta colors reflect off the ocean's surface; my mind captivated
by its brilliance will always reminisce on its utmost brightness.
Reflected magenta tears of joy, despair from
the fading twilight my soul annoys.
This sight no one could possibly forget, it is
the most unique and colorful sunset.
Now and forevermore will this breathtaking
sight within my heart endure.

ROMANCE

Be My Love

Won't you be my love? For I'll adorn you with the skies above.
I'll enclothe you with the mysteries of the stars. I'll hold
you close and love you from a distance if I am far.
Be my love and gleam of the dim moonlight. It'll
shine upon us as we dance through the night.
As the swaying winds brush through your hair, its
lovely beauty relieves me of my despair.
We'll travel as far as the farthest galaxy; we'll
start the most beautiful family.
As we search the skies from those that would do us wrong,
I'll serenade you each night with a beautiful song.
Be my love and come away to a hidden
place where we'll forever stay.
To you my love is forever sworn; with lights
and song, my beloved will be adorned.

A Day Without Light

The sun arose yet the world refused to shine. That is how
it feels in a world without you, both yours and mine.
Days go by, and the sunlight is absent in the sky.
The sun hangs low, but its appearance is depressing and dull.
Only by your presence does my day radiate and
glow. You are the only fulfillment to my soul.
The portrait painted by the sun is black and white.
Without you here, my day is long and without light.
Your smile radiates colors to the sky. Grass turns
green and flowers blossom as you pass by.
A day without you is like a day without light. The sun
may rise, but it always appears to be midnight.
If the sun shines without you, then to it I am blind. The
radiance of your smile is truly daylight savings time.

Beside the Sea

In my dreams we live so happily beside the sea, a happy
home with an extraordinary view from our balcony.
At night beneath the moonlight, we take barefoot
strolls upon the cool wet sand, gazing into each other's
eyes so lovingly while walking hand in hand.
Ebbing waves and a sandy beach as far as the eye can see,
you and I live together in a secluded home beside the sea.
Our only trouble throughout the day, choosing
from our favorite foods, I would say.
Early in the morning while we still yawn, we
awake just before the crack of dawn.
The sun rises slowly peeking from the east, we mindfully
enjoy the moment then proceed to feast.
With sticks and stones, we humbly build fires beside
the sea, we keep each other warm just you and me.
In my dreams we are each other's only needed company,
just the two of us and our humble home beside the sea.

Fingerprints Upon My Heart

Your hand has left fingerprints upon my heart;
colorful ink was used, and it shows in my art.
Fingerprints upon my heart have been recorded; my love
letters to you no matter the distance have been imported.
Your fingerprints will never be erased; they are my
only tattoos that could never be replaced.
Fingerprints upon my heart to paint you my beautiful
art; it is evidence to show that you stole my heart.
Your fingerprints left a most beautiful mark; starlight's
residue was used which is why it glows in the dark.
All fingerprints are unique, yet the touch of yours
are the only ones that make me feel weak.
Gently your fingerprints have left its mark on the world, a beauty
that will resonate for all time as long as the world continues to twirl.

Your Touch

Nothing is as warm as your embrace, or the warmth
that I feel at the sight of your lovely face.
That warmth could melt a snowflake, and the
touch of your hand is all it takes.
Without your touch, my heart is frozen; your touch is
like the dawn of spring that awakens all the roses.
Nothing is as lovely as the way you make me feel; your
touch is majestic that makes my wounds heal.
It mends my soul that is torn apart, and it lifts me
up to hear the sound of your beating heart.
Without your touch something is missing; I am
without purpose and hopelessly wishing.
Wishing for another moment, to awaken my
emotions that have gone dormant.
Nothing compares to your touch, aside from
that I really don't need much.

Midnight Sonata

A midnight sonata is played through the night,
by an endearing soul searching for light.
Serenades for a fire to continue to burn, each
note carefully and painfully learned.
Soulful singing tired and worn, seeking
strength to weather the storm.
A skillfully played instrument giving birth to romance,
as each listening heart learns a new dance.
Listeners learn a new song, through the
midnight hour making them strong.
A beautiful melody, in tune with the wind and uttered melancholy.
Rays of moonlight descend as they beam, echoes
of the sonata awake in your dreams.
A midnight sonata played for someone dearly beloved, it
falls unto deaf ears but mercifully heard up above.

A Taste of Your Smile

A taste of your smile would be so sweet; what a
day it would be when our lips finally meet.
Your smile is what draws me near; it is hypnotizing,
and your laughter is all I hear.
As you laugh and giggle, I can hear your
pain hidden beneath it just a little.
You hide it well; smiles bury it deep, but the
hurt I can see continues to dwell.
A taste of your smile would be a treat, ripe and
bright like a strawberry that is ready to eat.
As your smile curves and stretches your lips, I long for the
day when my arms are wrapped around your hips.
A smile that stretches for miles, resonating joy like that of a child.
Smile from ear to ear, it is your need for me that draws me near.

Affectionately Talking

We talk with affection, as we put on display every emotion.
You hear the words of my heart; our body language
makes music like that of a beautiful harp.
We forget all our worries. We are mindful of the
moment and have no anxiousness of hurry.
You look at me with affection. I hear every
word that you forget to mention.
A smile or tear from you tells me all I need to know.
I hear the deepest desires of your very soul.
Speak to me affectionately and let the blossoming
of our love be contemporary.
A loving affectionate kiss, filled with much passion and promise.
Under the rain that drizzles and drips, as do my tears
when I hear affectionate words from your lips.

Concepts of Love

If We Must

If we must, then let us acquire love through the conquering of lust.
For love and lust make us feel emotions that are very similar,
but each one has a completely different character.
Lust does not last, and its engulfing flame is brief,
what it leaves behind is long-lasting grief.
Lust is forged in one's imagination, love is formed
within one's heart leaving behind no aggravation.
Leaving hurt behind love does not, formation of lust
sprouts and blossoms from impure thoughts.
Lust is but a fiery thought, love is what since
the day of our birth we all have sought.
If we must choose, let us do so wisely so that
in this game of love we do not lose.
Though loud the echoing thoughts of lust, let us listen to
love's whispers within our hearts in which we trust.

Lovers' Quarrel

A painful lovers' quarrel, soothingly healed by the day of tomorrow.
Lovers' quarrels caused by sudden disputes,
sometimes it is better to humbly mute.
Arguments cause tempers to flare, with
disagreements that cause nightmares.
Often left wondering if the quarrel will ever be over, but
it will come to pass if you indeed are true lovers.
Jealousy is a toxic trait, there are trust issues
that make us question our soulmate.
A passionate kiss after a couple makes up, lack
of patience could lead to a breakup.
Quarrels caused by hearsay, one mustn't
leave angry but be patient and stay.
Much unnecessary sorrows, caused by an unnecessary lovers' quarrel.

Love's Language

For most of us love's language can be explained through
the explanation of a well-placed bandage, the reason
behind our mental and emotional damage.
Love's language can speak in many ways, translation
of a broken heart is depressive sorrow for days.
But love's language can also translate into an undeniable
beautiful smile; a vast vocabulary for your love's
language is through the gauntlet of fiery trials.
Our love's language can be explained through a
simple facial expression; if one listens carefully,
you can hear a heart's true intention.
Blindness nor deafness can silence love's language; a tight grip
must be used for love because true love will always be challenged.
Love's language is not mere words but continual
action; it is much more than physical attraction.
With kindness and support, love's language can be heard, and
I love you can be spoken silently even if that sounds absurd.
Love speaks with humility; love's language is a wholesome remedy.

Love Is

Love is often concealed, and tragically only
through heartache is it truly revealed.
Love is soft and tender, yet tough love is needed
so that it does not easily surrender.
Love is rare, true love is there before and
after the blossoming of gray hairs.
Love is not easily found, oftentimes it has to fight through
all the chaos to lift itself up from off the ground.
Love is not a mere word, but the continual
action of an ongoing verb.
Love is transparent, when love is gone it
becomes painfully apparent.
Love is needed, when one is drained and emotionally depleted.
Love is not found through a hug or a kiss, but through
continual kindness and support, this is truly love's gift.

Concept of Love

Most people have a misconception of what love is
or what it is supposed to be; for most, love is truly
blind because real love is hard for them to see.
A lot of people accept love through mistreatment,
instead of what it is supposed to be, endearment.
Love does not manipulate, to which too often most
relationships nowadays can easily relate.
Love does not accept manipulation, and if they do,
their concept of love is a misconception.
One can grow accustomed to the concept of love
that they've been shown, for some mistreatment
and manipulation is all they've ever known.
It is the love they've come to expect, sadly, it
is the love they've learned to accept.
And it becomes the love they come to offer, the
love they come to show unto others.
Most people love love's concept, but very few
show love's true nature of respect.

ROSITA

Rosita Grows

Rosita sprouts and blossoms from an itty-bitty seed,
she grows but is surrounded by briar and weeds.
Rosita's elegant rose petals, it deserves a new place to settle.
Rosita grows, but because of the briar and
weeds she is a poor lonely soul.
The rain descends upon her, as she absorbs the
rain she is nourished by the water.
Rosita continues to grow higher and higher; she
no longer fears the weeds and the briar.
Rosita has decided to own her place, she
won't let her beauty go to waste.
Rosita grows past the trees, her aroma is smelled
around the world, and she is finally free.
Rosita is no longer a poor lonely soul, her elegant
rose petals cast shadows upon the world even
though the process was painful and slow.

Rosita Sings

A most beautiful voice sings in the distance. It makes
me forget all the world's ugliness for an instant.
The voice is carried harmoniously by the wind. I
am filled with peace and love as Rosita sings.
Her voice is unique and quite like no other. She sings all
night and I ask, "Does she ever stop to take a breather?"
Rosita, you should sing for the world. I swear your
vocal cords are made of beautiful pearls.
Rosita, won't you sing for me? I'll write the newest
of songs, and you could sing it so peacefully.
You sing more skillfully than the skillful touch upon the strings of a
harp. It'll make rejoice even the most broken and saddest of hearts.
Rosita's voice is heard from miles away, as if she sings
from a mountaintop greeting the dawn of each day.
Rosita opens her mouth and releases musical notes. If you
were to sing for the world, your voice would echo throughout
history as it does in my heart from the last time we spoke.

Rosita Dreams

Rosita dreams consciously. She believes she will
see her dreams fulfilled eventually.
Many times before she has been robbed of her dreams. She has
shed many tears as through the night they continuously stream.
Anyone else would have already given up, but she
believes her desire to continue dreaming is enough.
Rosita works hard as day by day her dreams she cultivates and
nurtures. She believes she has something to prove for her culture.
Despite her nightmares that surround her like
scoundrels and vultures, she continues to see her name
in bright lights and her smile painted on posters.
Rosita through the darkest of nights endlessly dreams.
Stars are never too far away as upon her they gleam.
Rosita never stops dreaming. Her bright smile
always stretching and beaming.
No matter if she finds herself ill, Rosita is optimistic,
always believing in her internal will.

Rosita's Love

Rosita's love is a flame. Before and after it
kindled, my life hasn't been the same.
Her beauty leaves me in admiration. The radiance
of Rosita's rose petals is truly an inspiration.
Loving words from her lips, dew from her rose
petals nourish the earth below as they drip.
Lovely thoughts of Rosita that uplift my soul, reminiscing
on her uplift me when I'm feeling pretty low.
Rosita's love is the fire within me that still continues
to burn, my peace through the night without
which I would violently toss and turn.
Without Rosita's love, my heart would incessantly ache. I
admire her beauty through the night and gladly stay awake.
Rosita's love is much more than words can explain. It is
much needed just as a rose's growth is in need of the rain.
Rosita, where would I be without your love? The
aroma of your delicate rose petals is an incense
that reaches the heavens high up above.

Rosita's Song

Lights fell upon Rosita as they illuminate the stage.
Humbly and sweet, she read off the first page.
Music being played softly and melancholy, to
an audience as far as the eye can see.
Her innermost thoughts were being poured.
Listeners couldn't help but want to hear more.
So hurt and yet so passionate, the words she
spoke no one could ever forget.
She touched on heartache and healing. They were
topics that to many listeners was appealing.
She spoke of her struggles, and of all of her troubles.
For many it was difficult to believe. Others were amazed
by all the things she had accomplished and achieved.
She continued to read, trickling down her face were tearful beads.
Rosita shone under the bright lights. At her lowest low, she
could have never dreamed of reaching these pinnacle heights.
The audience was overcome with pang. They
commiserated with her as she sang.
Rosita was finally where she belonged. She eloped from her
impenetrable shell and finally let the world hear her beautiful song.
All night, she danced and she twirled. Indeed,
Rosita had left her mark on the world.

MEMORIES

Cherished Memories

These moments I cherish, more than the desires of a coveted wish.
These moments of friendship, when we feel closer
than two twins conjoined at the hip.
People in our lives come and go, but the important
ones we remember when we grow old.
Those that light up our day, we remember them
when our hairs begin to wither with gray.
Locked within our memories vault, we fondly
reminisce and defer to remember their faults.
It is said a friend can be closer than a brother, it must be
true because I would never replace you with another.
These moments I cherish, for moments with you to
my aching heart they rejuvenate and replenish.
One day from my presence you may be physically gone, but
the lasting memory of you to me will always be fond.

Forced to Understand

Years have come and gone since your passing, but
some memories we made are everlasting.
The earth we walk upon is not our eternal land, and
that is one thing death forces us to understand.
As life continues its never-ending course, one can
only choose to leave this land with no remorse.
In life we are forced to understand certain things, like
the painful moments that life along with it brings.
Years have come and gone since I saw you last.
My oh my, how time flies by us oh so fast.
I was forced to understand your presence in my life was temporary,
a short stint lasting shorter than the month of February.
As I grow old and memories begin to fade, I take
comfort in the memories that we made.
Time forces us to understand that life is short, and that
we cannot make it on our own without support.

Grief and Depression

Expression of My Depression

My poetry is an expression of my depression, but to
contaminate others with my depression is not my intention.
It is to show that out of the most remote places beauty
can appear, as skepticism can draw reluctance of fear.
My depression would not be expressed otherwise. If it
wasn't for my poetry, the only way you would know of
my depression is if you looked deep into my eyes.
Bottled-up emotional stress, many years of emotional
suppression is what has made me depressed.
Out of the cracks and crevices of my broken heart and mind, a rose
has sprouted and blossomed that for many years was confined.
The rose's aroma is unique. Its posture is unordinary and oblique.
The rose is the only hope that within me remains. The dew from
my tears is symbolic to what a rose needs to grow by the rain.
My poetry is an expression of my depression. It is an
artistic forging of my suppressed emotions.

Prison Blues

The hardest thing about being imprisoned is that life on the
outside goes on while you remain trapped; you are forced
to call life behind bars home, to which you must adapt.
Sons and daughters grow, while the hands on
the clock circulate extremely slow.
Mothers and fathers grow old, and the only embrace you
have are the iron prison bars that are always cold.
The dream of every prisoner is to one day be free from
the four walls in which they are confined, and to embrace
their loved ones for a momentary peace of mind.
The need of love is unfound, as chains
and shackles have one bound.
An imprisoned soul is broken; one's voice feels to go
unheard so one would rather remain unspoken.
Some prisoners commiserate with each other at times and
become friends; others remain hostile because the reality
of their imprisonment is difficult to comprehend.
Though by society prisoners are demeaned; an imprisoned soul can
be powerful if they don't lose their courage to continue to dream.

December in My Soul

December resides in my soul, freezing weather
due to the unrelenting snow.
Snowflakes gracefully descend; with undeserved
grace I wish to make amends.
It is my utmost desire, but I am at my wit's
end if only you were here to inspire.
December's absence of you makes it utterly cold,
bitterness is consuming which if not careful
could leave me with a permanent scold.
Heavy gusts of wind continuously oppress; it
makes my heart heavy inside of my chest.
An icicle hangs from the tip of my nose, yet I
continue to drag myself with heavy wet clothes.
Tears freeze as they trickle down my cheeks; unforgiving
blizzards have struck my life leaving me weak.
How I yearn for an early spring; a cold winter is
what December unfortunately brings.

Two Days in September

Two uneasy days, sometimes we must learn the harder way.
As fall begins the climates change, something in the air feels strange.
I feel it in the air, the burden of my heart's wear and tear.
I take it upon myself, choices made that are hazardous to my health.
Ones that brought instant regret, fortunately,
it wasn't time for my sun to set.
I feel and breathe my miracle, my laugh
after the sorrow is hysterical.
Realization of the change of season, is that
everything happens for a reason.
And for that I will always remember, even though it
was painful, my two dreadful days in September.

To Debbie

Absence of You

No words to express the emptiness of you not here. I
endlessly wander searching for you everywhere.
A once occupied space in the world is now left empty. Just one more
echo of your laughter would fill the vacancy in my heart plenty.
The world is a vast desert without a beginning or an end. It was
once a colorful pasture when it was walked upon by my friend.
Not even a shadow left behind, yet the resonating echo of
your voice continues to speak in my heart and mind.
Raindrops saturate the earth, a new heart
is formed and given unto birth.
Though the preciousness of a new life takes place, I still
see your beautiful smile stretched across your face.
In ambivalence I feel the sadness and joy of life
as it continues. A mysteriousness looms over me
as I wonder if I will ever again see you.
As I dreadfully trudge across this vast desert, the memory of you
remains alive even though your absence continues to hurt.

Unknown Pain

We all have unknown pain; unbeknownst to us,
it may leave us emotionally drained.
The pain of having grown up without a parent; only when
you've come of age does that pain become apparent.
This is the type of pain a child growing up suffers subconsciously,
and those stubborn tears if not shed will spew eventually.
Unknown pain of those empty spaces, I see
that pain even on unknown faces.
This emptiness painfully chips away; we are
unaware as we go about our day.
Unknown pain of nightmares unremembered; that
pain lingers within our hearts, right at the center.
The inability for some to shed a tear; it is torturous
because our soul the stream of tears we internally hear.
Unknown Pain, we all have it for we are all the same.

A Prisoner Cries

While all alone a prisoner cries, blessed to have a
window in his cell as he watches time fly.
He is awakened by the birds as they chirp; it is
soothing and slightly lessens the hurt.
The prisoner watches the dawn awaken, and he
is heartbroken because he feels forsaken.
Mindfully he feels the sun's warmth as he wraps his hands
around the normally cold window bars; there is no reason
to be hopeful, but he sees the sunrise from afar.
It momentarily makes him feel free; he takes a
moment to pray as he kneels on his knees.
At night he feels the cold midnight breeze; it reminds him
of the waves of the ocean and puts his soul at ease.
His imagination runs wild; his erratic thoughts
remind him of life as a child.
The only true freedom that he fondly remembers, sadly
now only recognized by society as a habitual offender.

Psychological Burden

At times I feel like a psychological burden to everyone
else; you would too if you've felt what I've felt.
There is mental stress; at times this makes
me feel like something less.
I don't profoundly believe it to be true; a psychological
burden could be what hinders you.
A burden that passes on sorrow, and its weight
because of the uncertainty of tomorrow.
An unbearable pain that makes me feel hopeless; the only thing
that could help relieve its weight is a neighbor's kindness.
Hopeful but filled with heartache, the pain
that derives all of my mistakes.
Sometimes pain and burden is psychological; gravity weighs
heavy on one, so you can say the pain is astronomical.
A psychological burden is a heavy load; to carry
this psychological weight one must be bold.

Gifted Liar

A gifted liar lies and slithers, not knowing that with
each little lie, they internally decay and wither.
They tell compulsive lies, meanwhile their soul slowly dies.
Not knowing their hiding from the truth,
internally hurting like a decayed tooth.
Lies are afraid of a challenge, gifted liars carry
internal wounds without a bandage.
A gifted liar unnecessarily lies, but the truth is revealed
by the burden bags of their sorrow-filled eyes.
They don't know that the truth shall set them
free, a rotten core like a bad apple tree.
But all hope is not lost, if they were to
search for the truth at all cost.
A gifted liar lies to him or herself, not knowing that the lies
they speak by everyone around is unfortunately felt.

Life of an Outcast

Life as an outcast of society, without many
options or choices in variety.
A life without much choice, so I search for a voice.
Poetry is my voice and only form of emotional expression.
After many years, it feels as if I am still in detention.
Still in the corner of the classroom, facing the wall and my
imagination running wild as daydreams over my head loom.
A friend of solitude, it is that that forges my attitude.
Longing to be truly accepted, which by my classification
as a mental health patient has been prevented.
I feel lonely and ghast, when I think about life as an outcast.
But my "ill" mind is befriended by my imagination. It leads me
to believe that there will one day be some sort of alleviation.

A Thousand Tears

If I cried a thousand tears, would you finally be able to hear?
The echo of my heart breaking, would it be awakening?
If that's what it takes, that might be my next goal to make.
To get to a thousand tears I think I'm halfway there,
but I want to know if you would even care.
A damp tissue, to help resolve my issues.
A waterfall from the window to my soul, my eyelids
try to protect me, but tears incessantly flow.
A piece of me drips to the ground, a thousand
tears being shed can be a deafening sound.
My emotions escaping from the cell in which they've been
confined, my tears being spewed for the sanity of my own mind.

Mindful Mourning

If you were to close your eyes, what would you
see? Perhaps a faint memory of me?
I closed my eyes, and you won't believe what I saw, a vision
of me surrounded by darkness as I hopelessly crawled.
What is a life without purpose? How is illumination
possible for a life that was forged in darkness?
I don't mean to sound abrasive, but this cold world for
me to behave any differently isn't too persuasive.
Why should I be humble? When the evasive light
continues to make me painfully stumble.
Why would you leave me in the dark? Robbing
me of my light, do you not have a heart?
I find myself in mourning, the deceased is
myself for I am gone without warning.
Everything hurts, my legs are not underneath me
for they are without strength and support.
I search for the bright side of things. I trick myself into
believing that my cup is half full, but I feel that I am lying.
As I look at the sky, I realize it is filled with
mystery and wonder. It feels unreachable as well as
incomprehensible, so I choose to slumber.
A temporary relief from my depression. I hate to
think of the thought of you as an obsession.
Obsessed with your presence, and sick at
heart because of its absence.

Sick all the way around; my heart, mind, and body, and I
just can't seem to pick myself up from off the ground.
Grounded beneath the dirt like a worm.
If only I had never been born.
Had I never been born, I would have never endured pain, but
the thought of having never existed also sounds insane.
Your love would have never been felt, lost in a realm
of nothingness with no one but myself.
The essence of my being would forever be a mystery.
Darkness would be my only known history.
I would not know dates or time. Complete silence
would be the sound of my doorbells chime.
My thoughts would be that of the dead, perhaps nothing
would be peaceful for my blood would have never bled.
My tears would have never been shed, and a hurtful
word towards me would have never been said.
I mindfully mourn, for myself, for my heart has been torn.
Painfully torn out of my sternum, yet my heart
continues to beat as loud as a drum.
The sound of my heartbeat is what keeps me going.
The sound of its echo is how I am surviving.
How much more could I possibly endure? Death and life
walk hand in hand and of which I prefer I am unsure.
A life for tomorrow is filled with uncertainty. Each breath
that I breathe is a testament that I've lived life valiantly.
I mindfully mourn until I find my life's value. I
mindfully mourn through my poetic blues.
Mindful mourning, for my fading candle to continue burning.

Footnote: If we entertain our negatives, there are always
reasons why we should give up. Equivalently there
are also much more meaningful reasons to continue
fighting. I speak on depression and the profound reasons
behind it to help myself and others overcome it.

HEARTBREAK AND REDEMPTION

Lethal Blow

You afflicted me with a lethal blow, and deep
down inside it wounded my soul.
But I am a man, and I will find a way to stand.
Lies can be lethal, especially when what you had was special.
I've been struck with lethal blows before, but I've
recovered and picked myself up off the floor.
Oh, the pain! It is enough to drive one insane.
The body trembles and shakes, and tears at night
make it hard to sleep for they keep you awake.
But the flame inside of me burns, and from the
lesson of this lethal blow I will learn.
And this lethal blow will not be my end, even though
I was struck by a dearly beloved friend.

Please... Please

I would crumble when I heard you say, "Please…please."
It was soothing and would put my soul at ease…ease.
But now I often wonder, so I ask her.
"Why must love knock on my door then leave…leave?"
The answer for this question I humbly plead…plead.
Love is carried away by the breeze. I am
reminded of it by the rustle of the leaves.
If love would only come back, please…please, because I refuse to
chase a runaway love because it only causes my soul grief…grief.
So before I lock love out and throw away the keys,
and because of love's absence I internally freeze.
I remember the sweet honey labored by the bees, and
I ask them, "May I have some, please…please?"
For of love's existence, I just want to believe, so of love's
presence in my life, I ask that you do not leave…leave.

In the Palm of My Hand

I once held the world in the palm of my hands;
it then turned to dust and slipped through the
cracks of my fingers like grains of sand.
I once revolved around the sun, but the sun grew
dark and weary, and it was no longer any fun.
Once the sun darkened the moon then ceased to illuminate,
and whatever joy that was left behind began to deteriorate.
The only hope I had left was in the stars, so I begged them
not to leave because that blow would be too harsh.
The constellation of stars now guides me; they've promised
me that never-ending light I will one day see.
The world I held in my hands was the shape of your heart;
its beauty only compared to the universe's celestial art.
Since the day my world fell apart, I wear tattered
garments and reside in the dark.
Your touch that was once felt in the palm of my hands,
will always have a vacancy for my world is your land.

Overnight

So strange how it grows utterly cold overnight.
Your smile towards me was no longer bright.
It is dull and plain. The sorrow it fills me with
draws tears like that of freezing rain.
You've grown cold, and all I can think about
is the lies that have been told.
A cold touch has made me emotionally numb. The night is
long, and I am anxious for the next day to finally come.
May tomorrow bring along with it some sort of
relief, for this sudden change of heart through the
night fills me with heartache and grief.
Overnight your eyes darkened towards me. Midnight was in
your pupils and the sparkle in your eyes I could no longer see.
Overnight your laugh was drowned by silence. Asphyxiation
came along with the cold atmosphere that suddenly grew dense.
Overnight we became estranged. I never knew the
midnight hours could so quickly bring change.

I Want to Be There

I want to be there, in the moments of hurt to show that I care.
In the moments when it is easier to run, when the daylight
is absent due to the disappearance of the sun.
When most people would turn their back and forget, let me be
one that continues forward without looking back with regret.
A love that has been painfully fought for, a
love that has brutally gone to war.
That is a love I want to share, to say that I stood
my ground that is a love I want to bear.
I want to be there to pick you up when you've fallen, when you've
made a mistake and the sparkle in your eye has darkened.
When the world is tired of hearing your tears,
I want to lend you a listening ear.
Into your tearful eyes I want to lovingly stare, when
no one else wants to I want to be there.

A Mended Heart

A mended heart can love more than one that's never been hurt,
for an unbroken heart has never had much love to exert.
An unbroken heart has never had to forgive, in essence
an unhurt heart hasn't much love to give.
Familiarity with heartbreak and suffering, allows
one to love with a love worth giving.
A mended heart makes love anew, a love
worth giving for me and you.
To truly love, some are fearful, perhaps because they've
experienced the downside of love which can be painful.
But a mended heart isn't something to fear, a
mended heart is something to be endeared.
It does not fear to make amends, or the
forgiving of an unthoughtful friend.
Mended hearts love with the weight of redemption, the
mending of a broken heart is love's true intention.

Taken for Granted

One's love is often taken for granted, and
treated as if that love was only rented.
That belittlement makes it difficult to open up, the reason
being that the emotions one reveals are difficult to discuss.
Emotions such as sadness or anger, the saddest part about it is that
those who take our love for granted are usually never by a stranger.
It is taken advantage of by those we love most, when all we
want to do is shelter those we love for our heart is the host.
We continue to forgive, sometimes we must
remember we have our own life to live.
With a loved one it is difficult to cut ties, we'd
rather mend relationships, but it is a difficult thing
to do when all they do is make you cry.
Sometimes we must simply move on, before the opportunity
of the beginning of something new is gone.
Some relationships are dead ends, sometimes
we must let go of a beloved friend.

Hey, Cinderella

Hey Cinderella, who runneth away from my love,
may I ask what it is that you are afraid of?
Why do you cut short our dance? You've left me with
happy feet in our short moment of romance.
I found your glass slipper, after a quarter past midnight
but you couldn't have left any quicker.
Now I am left searching for the one who can perfectly
fit this glass slipper, my neck from bending down trying
to find the perfect fit couldn't get any stiffer.
I yearn to rekindle the flame that lit our romantic night,
the flame that the wind blew away just before midnight.
The midnight's breeze carries your smell, always reminding me
of the night I fell hopelessly in love beside the wishing well.
Hey Cinderella, who runneth away with my love, who suddenly
sprouted wings and fluttered away like a graceful dove.
The wax melts and the flame flickers, and all that
I am left with is Cinderella's glass slipper.

Garden of Flowers
Hey, Cinderella 2

Oh, where has Cinderella run off? Nothing comparable
to the touch of her hand was as soft.
It is once again the midnight hour, and I painfully
sing sulking in this garden of flowers.
Moonlight on this particular night is absent. I admire
the flowers' beauty with the utmost reverence.
In the middle of the garden the glass slipper enshrined, the
midnight hour is hopelessly long, and I lose track of time.
All the flowers in the garden with sweet nectar drip.
They seem to cry with me as a tear hits my lips.
No one dares to draw near the glass slipper, a midnight
breeze, the name Cinderella gently whispers.
An endless sea of flowers, swaying with the
wind through the midnight hour.
The beauty of Cinderella forever etched in the garden. How
Cinderella's trample upon these flowers I wish to pardon.

Cinderella Returns
Hey, Cinderella 3

Cinderella returns, but the candle's fire no longer burns.
Underneath the beaming moonlight we go for a walk, she
explains her reasoning and hours pass by as we talk.
As Cinderella sniffles and weeps, my face is a stubborn
rock but internally my heart joyfully leaps.
She hopes I can find it in my heart to forgive, I
don't know whether to trust her for being hurt by
her again is not a pain I would like to relive.
I don't know if the apologetic words from her mouth
she truly means, her eyes have deceived me before,
but she did return like I had seen in my dreams.
I'd be lying if I said that to these burnt candles I didn't
want to rekindle the flame, tears begin to stream down
my face like window streams by drops of rain.
I'm hurt but the love I feel for her is greater, my
anger subsides by the tender lips of my lover.
Cinderella is finally home, and she takes a
seat at my side as I sit on my throne.

ELEMENTS OF TIME

Borrowed Time

Borrowed time slowly slips away, as the
clock continues to tick day by day.
The hourglass' relentless waves of sand, and
the clock's unstoppable hands.
Time is generous as it continues to loan, but the debt
is unpayable for it has doubled and grown.
Buzzers suddenly sound, at the time everyone gathers around.
Pendulums swing back and forth, as time speeds
towards eternity in an unrelenting course.
By everyone around time is unequally shared,
everyone runs out of time as no one is spared.
Time continues to tick, time is a dictator whose
everyone's final date it randomly picks.
A momentary shade eclipses the sundial, life is precious
but so often sadly wasted all the meanwhile.

Timeless

A single act of kindness, an action that in
another person's life can be timeless.
Forever remembered, when a kind gesture is rendered.
An engraved act of love upon a stranger, it can go a
long way upon a person whose life is in danger.
So we should look upon each other with a helping
hand, for life in the end will have its demands.
The demands of how we treat others, but we should
have no worries if we truly love one another.
So remember you could touch a stranger's heart with a single
word, and spring them into positive action like a single verb.
There is sometimes a mental illness, and other times a
person who finds themself in spiritual darkness.
It can be uplifted, and their outlook on life by
your kindness can be positively shifted.

Change

Change always comes; it is hard to deal with for some.
A lot of times necessary, change is inevitable
just as the end of the year into January.
Some things never change; if it did, life would feel strange.
Some change is internal, but fruits of that change
could last a lifetime or even eternal.
A change in our life could be sudden, in the blink of an eye
like an overcast on a sunny day that suddenly darkens.
But change can also be slow and grueling; it is sometimes
hard to deal with all the change that is ensuing.
For the need of change we are often aware, yet
we still go about our day without care.
Where and when is change coming? Sometimes it is right
before our eyes for change can be very cunning.

Test of Time

The test of time examines everyone; each individual
legacy if not careful will wither under the hot sun.
A legacy is not a legacy unless it's been tested, and the only way to
overcome that test is if to what we believe in we are truly invested.
Everything we are, needs to be polished so we shine like a star.
The test of time separates the good from the great; in the end,
those that believed will always know that it was their destined fate.
Destiny and fate go hand in hand as they peacefully
harmonize; long after a great is gone their
legacy and legend will continue to rise.
In the end when the greats look back and give themselves
a self-examination, with a microscopic lens that examines
the road that was paved towards their final destination.
Remembering the moments of solitude and silence; in the
end they will realize they were born with a sixth sense.
But to whom much is given much is tested, the test of
time is a necessary trial for those that are truly gifted.

Footnote: We all have a chance to be great.

Concept of Tomorrow

Today is everlasting, this moment the beginning of eternity. The idea of tomorrow is a belief we all have for tomorrow is just moments away. But in a single moment, tomorrow may forever remain estranged, a mystery that is never discovered. We all believe in tomorrow or the concept of it. And the concept of death seems unrealistic because we've never been personally exposed to death's clutches. Tomorrow is an illusion, and today, this moment, this single breath is all we have. Mindful of this moment and the appreciation of it is what makes life worth living. To be in the moment by looking loved ones in the eyes and speaking truth to one another is the breath of life. Tomorrow may never come, and subconsciously we are aware. But we take today for granted because of our conscious belief of tomorrow's certainty. Life can be sealed within the blink of an eye, for the moment we close it we are gone, and we become a memory that is slowly left behind. To leave a piece of us for the unfamiliar souls of tomorrow to be aware of our existence is not something many people can do, though none of us are ever truly forgotten as our soul continues to exist through eternity. For in God's ever watchful eye our past and future forever correlate with the present. The concept of tomorrow is an illusion and only this moment exists.

INSPIRATIONAL

The Caged Bird's Song

The caged bird sings because it wants to bestow the peace it once
felt as it freely flew, peace that it once felt it desires to see in you.
So the caged bird sings with grace, for since it is not free, it
wants to see the smile restored to your burdened face.
For the joy that the caged bird's song brings, it
momentarily feels the wind beneath its wings.
Remembering the freedom it felt when it used to fly, it does
not believe there is a purpose in seeing two beings cry.
The array of steel bars cannot hold back the caged bird's song,
so it sings hoping you momentarily forget all that feels wrong.
Passionately sung songs elope from within the cage, bringing
peace to the surrounding listeners' anger and rage.
The caged bird sings not only for its but your sake, with
intentions of your imprisoned smile to arise and awake.
Caged bird may you continue to sing; the purpose behind your
imprisonment is for all your listeners to one day also have wings.

Nothing Is Without Purpose

Nothing is without purpose; there is no life experience
whether good or bad that proves to be worthless.
In all aspects of life, moments of joy or moments of strife.
We should look to the greater beyond, that which
we cannot see of which we are quite fond.
Such as faith or hope, we cannot see these
things, but they help us cope.
Purpose for moments of pain, it enriches our soul
just as the earth is enriched by the rain.
For we are just glorified soil, for that very reason
we should not let our anger boil.
We are all in need of forgiveness, so though we hurt
and are hurt by others, there is a purpose.
Sometimes for that purpose to be revealed, all we have to do
is wait; the reasoning will soon come and surely not be late.

Late Bloomer

A late bloomer takes time to develop; many years are spent
scrounging until he or she finds the courage to stand up.
It does not necessarily mean the years beforehand were
a complete waste; sometimes it is a developmental
process for them to acquire good taste.
Oftentimes cocooned in a shell of self-doubt, self-examining
the depths of their mind trying to figure a way out.
A late bloomer may not seem much to the naked eye; they
spend many days sulking in depression wondering why.
Wondering if they'll ever finally bloom, it takes
courage to be a late bloomer as the thought of giving
up like a gray cloud always seems to loom.
A tenacious drive of will, all the meanwhile
others may think that they're mentally ill.
But a late bloomer in the end always flies, for their
birthright of living their dream never dies.
They may be late, but a late bloomer is always worth the wait.

Beautiful Mind

What creates a beautiful mind? Is there wisdom
in yours that we'd be able to find?
Creative thoughts that cause suspense, that
derive from a hidden sixth sense.
Thoughts that to others may seem absurd, but so
is the majestic ability to fly from a bird.
So we must search for new ways to create, before we are
buried with ordinary minds, and it becomes too late.
A beautiful mind transcends limitations,
exceeding personal expectations.
Whatever it is that is your occupation, to be something
greater is a beautiful mind's aspiration.
So our minds must continuously be fed, before
our minds are deceived and misled.
A beautiful mind could be inside of you; it is much needed
because beautiful minds in todays' society are very few.

What You Are to Me

You saw the pain inside of me, what all other eyes were blind to see.
When I was at my lowest, you resuscitated
the lifeless organ inside of my chest.
It is something I could never repay; my inability
to pay you back is in fact difficult to say.
At times I feel inadequate due to my problematic life that is
troublesome, but your much-needed touch is as gentle as they come.
Your love lifts me back to my feet; you are my second
wind when I feel overwhelmed and beat.
The inner strength that takes over me when I am
weak, my inner peace that I continuously seek.
You are my peaceful sleep's tranquility, and through
your eyes I see the heart of a lion inside of me.
The deep breath that I breathe so mindfully,
that is what you truly are to me.

Broken People

Broken people understand each other; they commemorate
their knowledge about what it is to suffer.
Though broken, by it they are not defined; their
brokenness allows them to be gentle and kind.
People that have suffered know what it is like to be hurt;
they know what it is like to be seen at your worst.
So when they see someone hurting, they understand, and
they are not hesitant about lending a helping hand.
For they know a simple act of kindness goes a long way;
they know an act of kindness can make someone's day.
Chronic thoughts of traumatic events circulate in their head; they
know the struggle of trying to find peace as they lay on their bed.
Broken people understand each other; they know survival
of their brokenness has only made them stronger.

To Diana G.

Hope's Song

Hope sings, my mind captivated by its musical
melodies after many days it continues to ring.
Hope within a broken heart is tightly concealed. It is the only
thing keeping it beating through all the pain that it feels.
The hopes of dreams and a purpose. It keeps the
broken heart from sinking into madness.
Hopes of seeing light at the end of a tunnel, for a lot of
the pain felt is not only within the heart but mental.
Hope continues to sing and through the dark tunnel it echoes. I
choose to follow it because I know whoever is singing is special.
Hopeful musical notes are played. Its
message of not giving up is relayed.
The song in the distance slowly fades. Darkness
engulfs me like a violent wave.
Still, I choose hope, for the hopeful song from
my depressive slumber keeps me woke.

Man of Few Words

When I was young, I used to talk a lot; it
made you cool or so I thought.
When I became of age, I became a man of few words. You
may think, You a man of few words, but that's absurd.
The words I speak are chosen, well thought-
out before they are ever spoken.
Still, I am a man of few words till this day, for
I listen before I say what I have to say.
Listening first can make you grow wise, instead of
entangling your tongue with deceit and lies.
Not everyone will take time to truly listen. My words are
meditated within my heart before they are written.
A man of few words but eager to speak, a paradox
because patience is the key to finding what I seek.
So please lend me your ear, as the man of few
words influentially speaks for a career.

Chronic Thoughts

We often have chronic thoughts that dictate our actions a lot.
Most of our thoughts are very repetitive; most of the time
they are bad or negative thoughts that make it hard to live.
Due to these chronic thoughts, we live with much distress; shame
or guilt oppress us and make these thoughts hard to confess.
We are often enslaved to these thoughts, by which
addictions into our lives are brought.
With hopes that these addictions bring us some sort of
relief, but the relaxation these addictions bring is brief.
After the short stint of a high, the chronic thoughts come back
worse, and the bad or negative thoughts retake their course.
The only outlet is through the long road of sobriety, which is
hard to do when these addictions are normalized in society.
Changing these chronic thoughts through a painful fiery
purge, will help us overcome our addictive urge.

Breaking the Cycle
Chronic Thoughts 2

Breaking the cycle of your thoughts can be a difficult thing
to do. It is something that can only be done by you.
Our thoughts usually have domain over our pain.
Thoughts are something of which we must ordain.
Or painful thoughts will continue to repeat, and the potential
to strengthen our minds will continue to be left weak.
Breaking the cycle of our thoughts through daily
cultivation, through daily structure and occupation.
Structure of our minds must be something we desire. Our
minds need to be fed like wood needs flame for a fire.
If not, ashes will cloud over our judgment, and
our potential will forever lay dormant.
Our minds have daily needs, for the cycle of
thoughts grows like unfruitful weeds.
Breaking the cycle of our daily thoughts must be something we
crave, or that same cycle of thoughts will take us to an early grave.

Special People

It is hard not to be embittered by the bitterness of other people,
but at the end of the day, that is what helps make us special.
Many people come and go from our lives, but on rare occasions
we meet those that change the very course of our life.
Special people are not born every day; certainly,
we are all special in our own little way.
Some people are meant to touch your life with a purpose,
perhaps to shed some light on you and save you from darkness.
It is uncertain as to what we perceive as what makes
someone special, but I believe it to be someone
who can easily relate to other people.
And not only relate but help them believe they are greater
than they truly are, for a single act of kindness goes very far.
There is nothing unordinary about special people
other than an empathetic character, for those are the
ones that can make your day feel spectacular.
Some people touch us in a way no one else ever has; they help
us realize and see the specialness about us that always was.

Footnote: Dedicated to all the special people who
saw the specialness in me before I could see it
myself. Anyone can choose to be special.

Please Don't Shoot Me Down

I am a bird flying through the sky; a bird
like no other, I like to fly high.
A bird that spreads its wings; every morning on
the highest treetop I relax, and I sing.
So please don't shoot me down, my city is sad, and
I just want to sing a new song for my town.
Like a bird that soars through the sky, I
am gentle before everyone's eye.
I am just a bird building his nest, so I can be
at ease and for my soul to find rest.
So please don't shoot me down, I just want to
see you smile and fix everyone's frown.
Like a singing bird, my damaged vocal cords can be heard.
So please don't shoot me down, I just want
to spread joy to everyone around.

Broken Crown

On my head there rests a broken crown. It is broken
because society is not yet ready to accept my place
in the world because my skin is brown.
My crown broke along the path I've traveled. It
broke yet shines so people are marveled.
I take a deep breath and mindfully hold the air in my lungs.
I let it go in blitzing anger, and I refuse to bite my tongue.
People are not ready for what they're hearing from
me. This broken crown gives me the de facto to
speak, and everyone will eventually see.
The crown rests on my once broken mind. The lost
and broken pieces took me a while to find.
The world is not ready to see a once broken prince. A broken
childhood and my smile has not been the same since.
A broken crown rests on my head. The brokenness
derives from where these broken roads have led.
A broken crown yet not defeated, scarred, and injured,
yet I stand while my enemies are seated.

Sad Girl

The sad girl was so curious; to the consequences
of her actions, she was so oblivious.
She proceeded to make mistake after mistake, and
often grew sad of the choices she made.
People would point and call her "sad girl," but deep down
inside, she knew she would one day change the world.
So she never thought of her tears as a waste, even
though her trail of tears left behind a bitter taste.
She sang through the midst of her sadness; it was her passion,
and it would get her through the midnight's darkness.
One cold and dark night, the stars heard her
beautiful voice; they said to her, "If you want to
become one of us, you must make a choice."
The sad girl said, "I know better choices I need to learn how to
make, but the love I receive in this world often feels so fake."
The stars said to her, "We know about the fake love you feel,
but the world needs to hear you sing. You must continue
to do so through whatever the world may bring."
Upon hearing those words from the stars, the girl's sadness
disappeared, and of the world's fake love she no longer feared.
So she sang until the sun came up, and from that day
forward, she believed her smile would always be enough.

Miss Sunshine
Sad Girl 2

After conversing with the stars, the sad girl no longer felt
demoralized and down, and everywhere she went, she
would smile and sing making such beautiful sounds.
People that knew her would ask amongst themselves, "Isn't
that the sad girl? She is scintillating as bright as a pearl."
She radiates and glows, they would say. They began to call
her Miss Sunshine because she shined as bright as midday.
Miss Sunshine of the world's fake love she no longer feared.
She knew her song the world would finally hear.
Everyone would rejoice, sing along, and cheer. And she would no
longer be known as the sad girl by her acquaintances and peers.
Miss Sunshine began to fight for her dreams in a daily
struggle. She began to pick up the pieces of her broken
life and put it together like an impossible puzzle.
Though at times her task would overwhelm her, she
accomplished her goals one day at a time believing
each day she was getting a little closer.
Miss Sunshine was indeed not the same person
as she was before. One day she would fly and like
a once broken eagle again finally soar.

The Awakening
Sad Girl 3

People that once knew the sad girl couldn't understand her
transformation. All the onlookers wanted an explanation.
They would ask and say, "Sad girl or Miss Sunshine,
why do you now radiate and glow? Is it because
deep down inside you are truly a kind soul?"
Miss Sunshine bewildered and perplexed, she smiled and said, "I
don't think my answer is something you would believe or expect."
The onlookers responded, "Miss Sunshine, don't leave
us in suspense." Suddenly the stars began to shine, and
the once frigid air was no longer cold and dense.
Miss Sunshine said, "It is because I speak to the stars up
above. They shine upon me and fill me with self-love."
Some were held in awe and to what Miss Sunshine had said
truly believed, others grew angry and began to leave.
Miss Sunshine grew sad at their disbelief, but instead of dwelling on
her sadness, she began to sing throughout the midst of her grief.
Stars began to ring as if they were angelic bells in
harmony. The music the stars and Miss Sunshine made
that night awoke the disbelievers consciously.

Painful Past
Sad Girl 4

Throughout the night filled with singing, Miss Sunshine grew
weary; she began having visions as if she was dreaming.
Or better said, nightmares; the people could tell something
was wrong, and they asked her, but she didn't want to share.
She was having a panic attack which she hadn't felt in
quite some time; she asked the scintillating stars for
answers to her dismay as she begged and whined.
The stars were faithful, and they provided answers to her weary soul.
The stars answered and said, "Beautiful girl, regressive
thoughts will often come, but if you believe, you
will always shine as bright as the sun."
Miss Sunshine felt warm, she felt comfort, but she remembered
how before she met the stars how her heart was completely torn.
She remembered that because of her shattered self-esteem,
how afraid she was to look in the mirror, and how every night
before falling asleep how her tears would run like rivers.
The dread of ever feeling that way again made her
decide that whatever it took to keep from feeling
that way again, she would diligently attend.

Coming Together
Sad Girl 5

After Miss Sunshine finally got some rest, she was back at
it again speaking to the stars and singing her very best.
Some people were happy for her while others were envious.
Miss Sunshine was aware for she was very meticulous.
She didn't want anyone to feel that way, so she began teaching
people how to speak to the stars throughout the day.
Her first lesson was to teach the people to be
humble. She said, "You have to believe in yourself
for the stars don't like it when you mumble."
The people were excited and eager to learn more. Most
people had never realized that for someone to listen to them
is for what their hearts had truly been yearning for.
In Miss Sunshine's beloved old town, depression
and sadness could no longer be found.
All the people soon realized that they enjoyed each other's
company. People that hadn't spoken to each other in years due to
old bitter disputes were singing beside each other in harmony.
Miss Sunshine and the people sang very loud, and
she cried tears of joy for she felt very proud.

A Star Is Born
Sad Girl 6

As the years passed, Miss Sunshine and the people
were doing better than ever at long last.
Miss Sunshine was no longer a young girl, and she had
accomplished her dream of truly changing the world.
Miss Sunshine was now old and gray, yet she
still shined as bright as midday.
She shined but at times felt physically weak. One
night while all alone the stars began to speak.
They said, "Wise woman, the time approaches for the
sun to finally set." Miss Sunshine grew slightly fearful
but trusted the stars for she knew what they meant.
One night as the people were in assembly, Miss Sunshine
began to speak to them kindly and gently.
She wanted to sing a new song. The people
loved it and began to sing along.
By the end of the song, Miss Sunshine laid face up and flat on
the ground. The people grew quiet and wouldn't make a sound.
Suddenly a star high above all others shined brighter than any
of the people had ever seen, and they realized Miss Sunshine
had become one of them, finally fulfilling her dreams.

Talk of the Town
Sad Girl 7

Even after death, Miss Sunshine was the talk of the town, for
her funeral she was dressed in a bright-yellow evening gown.
It was befitting; it complimented her natural glow
everyone thought as they were singing.
Miss Sunshine had been eternalized, so ironic for
a person who once lived so demoralized.
Everyone sang her songs, and the new star
radiated and shined all night long.
Even those that knew her best were in awe and disbelief; they were
filled with joy at Miss Sunshine's passing instead of sorrow and grief.
No matter where you went in Miss Sunshine's old
town, you could not find a bitter old frown.
Miss Sunshine had accomplished what she never
thought possible, and everyone's joy was palpable.
Miss Sunshine was truly loved, and dearly
missed as she was received up above.

The End…

Method to the Madness

There has to be a method to the madness, just as
there is always light in the midst of darkness.
Though the methods do not always seem to make
sense, and at times they can make us feel tense.
We must realize revolutionary ideas have always taken extreme
methods, but the impact that comes from the message,
It is always worth the wait, and it soon becomes clear that
the painstaking process has always been one's fate.
The methods needed to reach one's destiny,
will become apparent eventually.
Though the process may not feel quick,
And at times throughout it we may even feel sick.
We must trust in the method's madness; in the end, it will
feel as if our accomplishments were acquired flawless.

I Know

I know what it is like to be forgotten, but destiny arises
in the horizon as the dusk's twilight is begotten.
Though some of my hardships were undeserved,
grace and destiny humbly serves.
I know what it is like to be hungry, and what
it is like to panhandle for money.
The embarrassment that you feel, it is humiliating
so at times you'd rather steal.
I know what it is like to be homeless, a cold feeling of abandonment
and your only companion is the seed of your dream's brightness.
So you offer a prayer, for in those lonely hours
you realize you're in need of a savior.
I know what it is like to suffer, but the survival
of it only makes you tougher.
I now finally know it was all these experiences that helped me grow.

Death on the Battlefield

A soldier dies on the battlefield; his sword
and his shield he no longer wields.
Weary and body exhausted, a lifelong battle he brutally fostered.
In the end, he claimed his prize, many rose at his demise.
A fulfilling death because before his eyes closed
they saw victory, and his achievements don't go
unrecognized as he takes his place in history.
An unrecognizable wounded torso, with an
equivalent beaten and battered soul.
Though his body is gone his name never dies, many
are left in wonder at his sudden goodbye.
His brutal love's labor, to bestow upon his loved ones a blessed favor.
Though his blood upon the land was tragically poured, he
fought his fight to the end and never relinquished his sword.

Voice of Reason

The voice of reason, it speaks to me
throughout the different seasons.
Through the cold, "I am your fire," I was told.
When it is hot, it said, "I am the shade that you sought."
In the fall, the voice of reason continues to call.
In the spring, the voice gives me courage to sing.
The voice of reason has been with me through the winter,
it comes from within my heart's very own center.
Despite the summer's heat, the voice of reason continues to speak.
This voice gives me reason, forever with me
through the hot and cold seasons.

Bad Influence

At a young age, I was labeled by my teachers as a bad influence,
which at that age in my mind it was difficult to make sense.
To many teachers, I was their greatest fear. I infected
others with rebellious behavior, and for that reason,
I was frequently isolated from my fellow peers.
These isolations were where my vivid imagination began, that
imagination slowly molded me into the poet that I am.
Being labeled as a bad influence made me feel as if I
should live up to my potential, so I became the class clown
because I had a great act, and I put on a great show.
I was expelled from three different schools. Most
teachers probably thought I was a fool.
And for a long time I did too. I reflected as an adult
and realized it was never me being a fool but because
the surrounding positive influences were very few.
No one ever taught me how to effectively study on my own,
so studying wasn't a priority whenever I was home alone.
My poetry derives from hours of self-education. A
lot of questions that I had in my adolescence were
answered by my own research's explanation.
Hours of my life as an adult were spent in the local
library. The subjects I studied always varied.

It was a difficult process to shake myself from today's
normalized illiteracy. When I embarked on a personal
quest for knowledge, I felt as if somebody didn't want
me to discover the power of education's golden key.
So even though for a long time I was a bad influence, irony
harmonizes effectively, and my broken path makes amends.
And now I finally have something I can call my own,
for in the world of literature I have found a home.

"Mentally Ill"

If there is a hope I could instill, to all those
lives that are considered mentally ill,
it is that your illness does not define you, and
that life after a diagnosis continues.
I know it is hard to believe in an illness that cannot be visibly
seen, so you pinch yourself hoping that it is all a terrible dream.
You feel as if no one can relate, and every conversation
about it feels to be an argument or debate.
So you choose to bottle it up, but this is the worst thing
you can do because those emotions will one day erupt.
You just need to find people in whom you can confide,
people you trust that'll never leave your side.
There are still people in which you can find comfort,
to help you relieve and lessen the hurt.
Don't bottle up the stress, the hurt you feel needs to be addressed.

Successful Failures

We all have failures; they are not easy, they
make us doubt, and feel unsure.
Especially when our goals are unmet, but a successful failure is
all about how you look at a situation; if you become fearful of
failing again, you will become fearful of future confrontation.
A potential learning experience arises from each one of
our failures; if the lesson is learned, it can be a cure.
An unsuccessful failure can leave us paralyzed; if we take
time to closely examine our past failures, we may see that
it was more successful than we initially realized.
A successful failure is only seen through the agonizing trial
of patience, for failure is a very humbling experience.
It takes time for a successful failure to produce its
fruit, but only through the eyes of humility can it be
seen otherwise we can become prideful brutes.
Successful failures are valuable lessons; they teach us more than
we could have ever learned from immediate success in the end.

EQUALITY

Poetic Justice

Poetic Justice cries out, people crying for justice let off a shout.
A hand upon our heart to show our patriotism,
yet there is no war going on to end racism.
Bloody stains make us cry upon our land, of
unanswered justice left in our leaders' hands.
So unanswered justice is answered by angry riots,
the winds of change can be felt in the climate.
Poetical cries heard from teardrops as they hit the ground,
yet political leaders refuse to acknowledge the sound.
How much more blood and tears must be shed? Is there
really a need for our land to continue being painted red?
Officials undeclared war on minorities, why can't justice
be carried out upon all with the same symmetry?
So poetic justice continues to cry, as to our loved ones
we must heartbreakingly continue saying goodbye.

My Skin

My skin, beautiful and brown, a thick skin
for all the chaos that surrounds.
While I bask under the hot sun, it becomes bloodstained
red like my ancestors; sweat drips from the countless
miles I've walked throughout all my ventures.
My skin is gifted to me by a Salvadoran bloodline; in the
summertime, it is as if I've coated myself with a coat of red wine.
Brown pride, when I was a child, society made me
feel that it was something that I had to hide.
My skin is brown as if I've been molded by dirt, for I've
been stepped on so much that I still feel the hurt.
Brown skin that shimmers with sweat, just like my mother
that has the most beautiful skin that I've ever met.
Pride in our beautiful brown skin in today's
generation has become rare, for we waste our youth
on stereotypical expectations without care.
Blessed with brown skin and honor, yet I bleed
red like every other different skin color.

Apples and Oranges

What is the difference between you and I? We both smile and
cry, and at one point or another, we have both told lies.
Aside from the difference in skin color, we
look exactly the same as our neighbor.
Some are short and others tall; we all need
a helping hand when we fall.
All of us were born of a woman; so what's the difference
between an apple, orange, or even a lemon?
Where is the difference found? All of us are but
dust that'll one day return to the ground.
So why treat me indifferent? For the hate you give
consumes the life that is but a short stint.
Differences can be found within our character, for
the hate you give within my heart is unfamiliar.
Apples and oranges are but fruits to eat; you and I are
strangers but both of us our maker we will one day meet.

Different Colors

You and I are similar and a lot like each other,
tall and short but of different color.
We both feel sadness and joy the same; the color of our
skin shouldn't bring along with it guilt or blame.
I cry and shed tears just like you; if we were
color-blind, you'd know this to be true.
Colors should not dictate how we behave; in
our hearts is where beauty is engraved.
Poor character should be the only judgeable stain,
for the color of our skin cannot be ordained.
You cannot fix what isn't broken, and we can
only see this with our eyes wide open.
My skin is not better or worse, but I am
proud of who I am with no remorse.
Everyone around us is unique and of different color, but that
does not mean we cannot live in peace with one another.

Creative Writing

Emotionally Dancing

A sad and gentle soul dances with happiness, the
joyful dancing relieving all the stress.
Courage found in the midst of oppressive fear,
resilience of bravery makes one endeared.
Anxiousness was done away by surprise, eyes
reluctantly opened up so wide.
When the music stops the same calm and gentle soul,
cannot wrap its head around the depressive lows.
Emotions dance on and on, burning desires have
their toes stepped on until the fire's gone.
So the soulful dance must enhance, until
destiny emerges from the romance.
Everyday emotions within fulfill, surrounded by triggers
of music which is why happy feet cannot stay still.
New dances emotionally take form, the fire burning
and the gentle soul now feels warm.

Inspired by Mo

Deep Speaks unto Deep

Deep speaks unto deep; this is evident when
a vivid dream arises as we sleep.
Mysteries of a man's spirit, when it awakens in the
dream realm through a nocturnal vision's visit.
We do not always see what is before us, but we
sometimes sense things that are difficult to discuss.
Difficult because we fear what others may think; when we realize
we were not wrong, our hearts begin to slowly churn and sink.
The depths of our very soul, cries out as the
mysteries of tomorrow are foretold.
It is said blood is thicker than water; if we know this, then
why when blood proves its dominance are we bothered?
It is because deep speaks unto deep, and in the
depths of the ocean blood disperses as it seeps.
When a truth is revealed, the depths of our hearts are forever sealed.

Paradoxical Reality

The sun shines yet it is dark, fire burns yet there is no spark.
I smile on the outside, but I am flooded by tears on the inside.
I scream as I drown, yet there is no sound.
I've given up, but I've not had enough.
The days are long, yet they are quickly gone.
My heart's lonely ache, yet everyone commiserates.
My head is in the clouds, but I fall to the ground.
A paradoxical reality, a peaceful calamity.

Poetic Freestyle

Clever endeavors to remember, fall during the midst of September.
Searching the depths of my mind, trying to
find a reason to continue being kind.
Hurt and unappreciation makes the roads foggy, but
the thought of you reminds me to behave kindly.
In a cold, cold world, a frozen acorn is
relentlessly pursued by a squirrel.
Societies ice age type weather, it has me wondering
if we as a whole will ever get better.
On a daily basis bodies are being outlined by chalk
like a stencil, it makes it easy for my tears to drip
from my eyes to the tip of my pencil.
Poetic writing is my outlet, but a stress-
free heart I wonder if I will ever get.
This is a poetic freestyle, which brings to my face a temporary smile.

Melody of My Soul

A newborn's cries, it is the melody of my soul in disguise.
Crying at the bright lights and the unknown,
the welcoming of a new home.
Continual dripping of tears is the sound of my soul's
melody, your awareness of my cries is my only remedy.
Imprisoned tears have me slowly deteriorating,
but my soul's rhythm is liberating.
The melody of my soul is unique, it is only heard
when I am overwhelmed and weak.
Musical melodies can be heard from afar,
my soul's melody reaches the stars.
A newborn's cries by everyone around is heard, their
message is relayed without the speaking of any word.
A newborn's cries is our very first song, my soul's melody
within your heart is right where it belongs.

Creation

Creation, it starts with love, a neglection
to anything we may be fearful of.
Sacrifice of one's kingship, loving words uttered by unhesitant lips.
Creation unfolds, only by words that are truthfully told.
Unforeseen lights sprout from the realms of darkness, as
the universe expands from a humbled heart's kindness.
Only by one who is willing to sacrifice, only then will
eyes be unveiled to an unparalleled paradise.
Granted by an eternal mercy, hidden within an existence of secrecy.
An existence that eyes cannot foresee, only by
those whose faith is guarded closely.
Creation of which we have no explanation,
by a love that had no hesitation.

The World Is a Stage

We've been auditioning since the day we were born; in
the end, we will be judged on how we perform.
The world is a play; its dramatic scenes unravel day after day.
The world is a stage, scripts filled with ups
and downs on page after page.
Characters and plots, as the ultimate
treasure is continuously sought.
Filled with heartache and joy, some scenes are hard to enjoy.
Others we'd love to watch again and again; mysteriousness
forever looms above us on how it will end.
When the curtains finally close, at our feet may there be a rose.
As the world awaits its final act with great anticipation,
in the end, may we have a standing ovation.

Footnote: Inspired by an actual dream

Alcatraz Bars

Alcatraz Bars are being spit. Penitentiary flow let off some hits.
Cold iron bars, but I take the warmth from the stars.
Behind these iron bars I have been cut. The sound
of them is traumatizing as they open and shut.
These cuts have left internal scars. In my Alcatraz there is no yard.
My bread is stale, my water is bitter, it makes me turn pale.
Despite all this I've not given up, a nail file
is my cake. I will make my escape.
This is a penitentiary flow, from a suffering addicted soul.
But these cold iron bars will not break me down. On
my head there will be placed an honorable crown.

Distributor of Karma

The distributor of karma equally gives everyone shares;
we recognize it at times but don't seem to really care.
Karma is not a self-sufficient verb; an outstretched arm hands
it out so that from our actions we may one day learn.
It is not sent with the purpose of breaking us
down, but rather lifting us up so that we may
become better people all the way around.
The distributor of karma hunts those who have bitten the forbidden
fruit, so that we may pluck our sin from deep within its roots.
Though bad karma inflicts on us pain, its purpose
is to cleanse our soul from its sinful stain.
The distributor of karma wouldn't send it out after us if he didn't
care, even though the fruits of karma are ours alone to bear.
Karma is the distributor's discipline, to
correct us from the way of our sin.
It is always humbling to receive correction, but the distributor
hopes that from it we learn as growth is karma's true intention.

Life's Journey

A life without direction, it cannot have a great end expectation.
Life's journey is unpredictable, finding
reason at times feels unexplainable.
Life is uncertain, it is unbeknownst to us
when life may close its curtains.
Appreciation of the breath you breathe, for one
day that last breath will certainly leave.
Then we will not have time to look back on what has been left
behind, our appreciation of life is a key to peace of mind.
Life's journey has its final destination, and the questions
to life's mysteries will one day have its explanations.
Life's journey takes each one of us through our own
route, along its course our job is to water the seed of
knowledge so that it may take root and sprout.
So that we may leave a map to the next weary soul's
quest, as we are finally laid to our eternal rest.

What Is a Dream?

What is a dream but a forged subconscious echo of
thought and imagination? Dwelling deep within
your mind developed for a new creation.
What is a dream's purpose? But to awaken us
from a weary shut eye's darkness.
Dreams lead us to our future goals, to awake
our slumbering and wandering souls.
What is a dream but a subconscious figmentation, and what of
the attributes of a dream that lead us to feel a physical sensation?
Why is a dream needed? But to lift us when we're feeling defeated.
There are supernatural effects of a dream that places
us in a familiar situation, concocted by the aware
subconscious efforts of our imagination.
What is it to dream with our eyes wide open? It is a tunnel vision
that grasps our destiny so that our dreams do not leave us forsaken.
Why do we dream? But to arouse us from a deep sleep,
so our destined destiny may one day be achieved.

The Greatest Untold Story

In the realm of purgatory, William Shakespeare once
said to Edgar Allan Poe, "Let's collaborate. We'll make
the greatest poem ever." Poe said, "The stories about
you were not just tales for that idea is quite clever.
The problem is we are polar opposites." Shakespeare
said, "That is why we are the perfect fit."
"What do we write about?" asked Poe. Shakespeare said,
"Love, tragedy, and things that touch people's souls."
Poe said, "That sounds superb. I'll begin on your word."
Shakespeare said, "Unwelcomed shadows and dark figures…"
Poe said, "…rob me of this ring on my finger."
Shakespeare said, "My shadow, my only faithful friend…"
Poe said, "…only with me his time he chooses to spend."
Shakespeare said, "The day is long…" Poe said, "…oh,
but I think that you're wrong for yesterday is gone."
Shakespeare said, "The height of heaven's pinnacle is only
obtainable after you've known of the tragic tales here down below."
Poe said, "The only ones who know are the heartbroken souls."
Shakespeare said, "Love will find a way to conquer…"
Poe said, "…if only I was a little bit stronger."
Shakespeare said, "Your strength alone is enough." Poe said,
"But I've had it rough, and the road ahead is just too tough.
No love stronger than Romeo and Juliet, and not
even they conquered, did you forget?"

Shakespeare said, "I have not, but Romeo and
Juliet is not the end that you thought."
Poe said, "Explain so and elaborate to my perplexed soul."
Shakespeare said, "Their tragedy inspired countless future lovers.
The thought of their names alone has made countless hearts flutter."
Poe said, "Lessons on patience and communication, but why did
such tragedy have to occur for us to receive an explanation?"
Shakespeare said, "No one truly knows, but their tale
has brought together many wandering souls.
Even the raven knows of your dear Lenore. And how
the love you gave her is with her forevermore."
Poe said, "Of that I am aware, for her heart and mine have
intertwined and our love and heartbreak are forever shared.
For the night the raven knocked on my chamber door,
as I cried and wept cold and broken on the floor.
It made me realize that she felt the same way wherever
she was as I could see her through the raven's eyes."
"You see, Poe? There is always hope," said Shakespeare. Poe said,
"Thank you, as you have done away with my greatest fear."

Masterpiece

I write and compose, inspired by heartache, I suppose.
It is a masterpiece, all while overwhelmed by grief.
But I write to inspire, for listeners to pursue their utmost desire.
We all have but one life to live, and if we end it
with regret, it would be difficult to forgive.
So I hope listeners fight for what they long for most,
something that is truly worth one's boast.
We all have our own masterpiece to create, and its creation will
have onlookers with something in which they could easily relate.
A true masterpiece dwells within; it takes time to be
unveiled, but it's been present since before our origin.
The brightness of our soul's creation, it carries a
masterpiece, we just need to find the inspiration.

Footnote: We all have our own masterpiece to create!

The Last Sunset

What of the beauty of the last sunset? A radiance of all bright colors. The beauty of all autumn leaves painted in the sky by tears from the sun. Sadly, it slowly then suddenly declines. Such is life, but a temporary beauty. Nature slowly dies; the once fluorescent moon is left lonely. The sky is dark and no longer blue, dimly lit by distant glimmering stars. Humanity reminisces on the last sunset; its captivating final act was one to remember. Forever etched and engraved in the hearts and minds of those who saw it. All is not lost as long as there is one to remember and pass on the knowledge of a once brightly lit world thereafter. A breathtaking sight that captivated all beholders, the world without the sun's warmth is a lot colder. Survival is uncertain, but if one were present that remembers the lessons of the persistent sun that continuously lit a dark world, they will remember that the darkness is not an eternal dwelling place to a persistent soul that like the sun continues to rise. And that the seemingly eternal darkness that has taken the last sunset's place will once again find a way to shine. The skies far and wide will find a way to bloom with the blueness of the ocean, and the forgotten warmth of the sunshine will find a way to envelop our sadly cold world. The last sunset will forever shine in the hearts of those who remember the true Picasso in the sky.

About the Author

Josue Rios was born December 17, 1989. For the most part, he was raised in Manassas City, Virginia. He grew up very close to his mother, brothers, and sisters. He's made many lifelong friends from the schools he attended, including Osbourn High School where he received his GED. In school, he was always in constant trouble resulting in expulsion. Josue never went to college but did a lot of studying on his own accord after high school at local libraries, where he developed his writing ability over the years. There were times when he thought he was wasting his time going to the library and studying, but he kept at it. He never expected to become a published poet, but he enjoyed writing poetry, and one day the number for a publishing company fell onto his lap. Josue reached out to the publishing company, and the rest became history. Josue hopes to inspire those who feel they have lost their way or the ones wandering without direction. And he is hopeful that his poetry will do just that!

www.ingramcontent.com/pod-product-compliance
Lightning Source LLC
Chambersburg PA
CBHW061346160726
47995CB00001B/194